The Life of a
SALMON

Clare Hibbert

www.raintreepublishers.co.uk
Visit our website to find out more information about **Raintree** books.

To order:
 Phone 44 (0) 1865 888112
 Send a fax to 44 (0) 1865 314091
💻 Visit the Raintree Bookshop at **www.raintreepublishers.co.uk** to browse our catalogue and order online.

First published in Great Britain by Raintree, Halley Court, Jordan Hill, Oxford OX2 8EJ, part of Harcourt Education.
Raintree is a registered trademark of Harcourt Education Ltd.

Editorial: Nick Hunter and Catherine Clarke
Design: Michelle Lisseter and Tipani Design
   (www.tipani.co.uk)
Illustration: Tony Jones, Art Construction
Picture Research: Maria Joannou and Ginny
   Stroud-Lewis
Production: Jonathan Smith

Originated by Dot Gradations Ltd
Printed and bound in China by South China Printing Company

ISBN 1 844 43316 1
08 07 06 05 04
10 9 8 7 6 5 4 3 2 1

British Library Cataloguing in Publication Data
Hibbert, Clare
The Life of a Salmon. – (Life Cycles)
597.5656
A full catalogue record for this book is available from the British Library.

Acknowledgements
The publishers would like to thank the following for permission to reproduce photographs:
Ardea pp.**13** (P. Morris), **15** (P. Morris), **17** (Chris Martin Bahr), **24** (Francois Gohier); Corbis p. **9**; FLPA pp. **5** (David T. Grewcock), **20** (Foto Natura), **21** (Gerard Lacz); Getty Images pp.**4** (National Geographic), **10** (Stone), **19**; Jason Hawkes Aerial Photolibrary p.**18**; Natural Visions pp.**11**, **12**, **16**; NHPA pp.**8** (G. Bernard), **23** (Kevin Schafer), **25** (John Shaw), **26** (Trevor McDonald), **27** (Jean-Louis Le Moigne), **28** (Dan Griggs); Science Photo Library (Art Wolfe) p.**29**; Woodfall Wild Images pp.**14** (John Robinson), **22** (Sue Scott).

Cover photograph of an atlantic salmon, reproduced with permission of Oxford Scientific Films (Keith Ringland).

The publishers would like to thank Janet Stott for her assistance in the preparation of this book.

Every effort has been made to contact copyright holders of any material reproduced in this book. Any omissions will be rectified in subsequent printings if notice is given to the publishers.

The paper used to print this book comes from sustainable resources.

Contents

Any words appearing in bold, **like this**, are explained in the Glossary.

The salmon

Salmon are a type of fish. Like all fish, they live in water. They have smooth, scale-covered bodies with fins that allow them to swim. Like you, they need to breathe in a gas called **oxygen**, which they take from the water using **gills** – special body parts found under slits on the sides of their head.

Salmon babies hatch from eggs that are laid in freshwater streams and rivers. As adults, they spend most of their lives in the sea.

These adult salmon are swimming in the ocean.

eye　　gills　　fin　　tail

Growing up

Just as you grow bigger year by year, the salmon grows and changes, too. The different stages of its life make up its **life cycle**. There are different types of salmon and they all go through the same life stages.

Where in the world?

Adult salmon live in the oceans. There are two main types – the Atlantic salmon lives in the Atlantic Ocean and the Pacific salmon lives in the Pacific Ocean.

When baby salmon first hatch, they do not look much like their parents.

A salmon's life

The **life cycle** of a salmon begins in spring, when salmon eggs hatch in streams. The young fish live in rivers and **estuaries** for one to three years. The salmon then **migrates**, or travels, to its ocean feeding grounds. It spends up to eight years at sea, slowly gaining weight. Finally it is fully grown and ready to **spawn** – lay eggs that will develop into new salmon.

Making young

Both males and females leave the sea to make the long, dangerous journey upstream to their **spawning grounds**. The female lays her eggs in a stream. Most salmon die a few days after spawning.

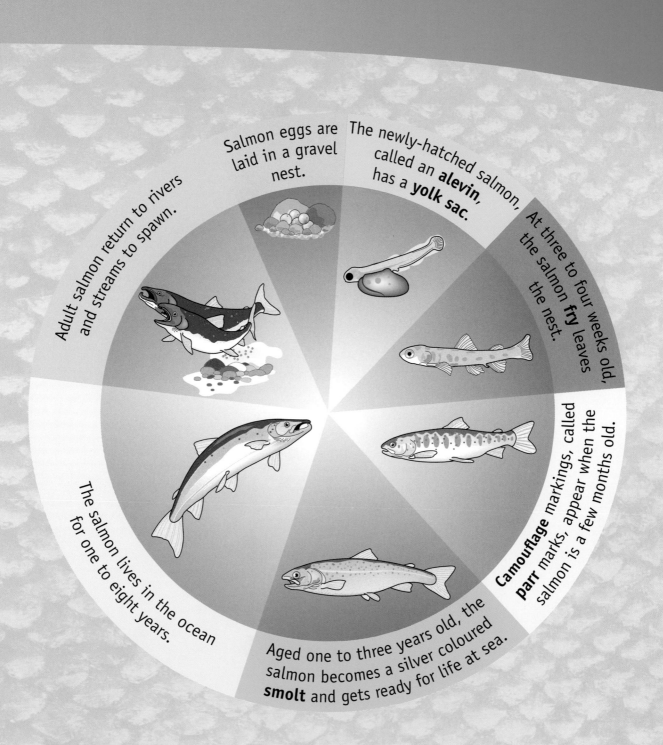

Salmon eggs are laid in a gravel nest.

The newly-hatched salmon, called an **alevin**, has a **yolk sac**.

At three to four weeks old, the salmon **fry** leaves the nest.

Camouflage markings, called **parr** marks, appear when the salmon is a few months old.

Aged one to three years old, the salmon becomes a silver coloured **smolt** and gets ready for life at sea.

The salmon lives in the ocean for one to eight years.

Adult salmon return to rivers and streams to spawn.

This diagram shows the life cycle of a salmon, from egg to adult.

A watery nest

The female salmon lays her eggs in streams that have bubbling water. She buries the eggs in a shallow, gravel nest called a **redd**.

The eggs need cool, clean water. Shady trees along the bank stop the water becoming too warm. The gravel nest lets through water, which washes around the eggs and keeps them clean.

Healthy salmon eggs are pinky-orange in colour.

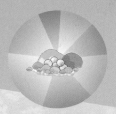

Survivors

Not all the eggs survive. Sometimes a redd is destroyed by people or animals crossing the stream. Sometimes the eggs die because conditions are not quite right. Eggs that have died turn a milky-white colour. Inside each healthy egg a baby salmon, or **embryo**, is developing. After two months, it is ready to hatch.

Egg eaters

Although they are hidden under the gravel, some of the salmon eggs are sniffed out by hungry hunters. Crayfish and trout love to snack on salmon eggs.

Crayfish live in freshwater lakes, rivers and streams. They eat salmon eggs, fish, insects and water plants.

Hatching

It is early spring. The salmon eggs are about to hatch. Newly-hatched salmon are called **alevins**. Each is about 2–3 centimetres long and has a balloon-like bag hanging from its body. This is its **yolk sac**. It contains enough food for the alevin to survive for about a month.

Each alevin has its own food supply – a yolk sac attached to its body.

Home, sweet home

The alevin stays in the safety of the **redd**. Its body needs to become stronger, and grow fins so that it will be able to swim. For now, the alevin can only move short distances by swishing its tail from side to side.

Teething

While the alevin is soaking up the yolk sac, its body is getting ready for life outside the nest. Inside the alevin's mouth, sharp teeth begin to push through the gums.

As the alevins grow, their yolk sacs get smaller. That is because the young fish are slowly using up the food.

Small fry

After three to six weeks, the **alevin** has used up its **yolk sac.** Now it is called a **fry.** It must swim out of the **redd** and hunt for its own food. At first, it feeds on **microscopic** animals and plants. As it grows bigger, it eats insects that live in the water. The fry grows scales all over its body. Scales are like a suit of armour that protects the fish.

The salmon fry swims out into the stream.

Beginning a journey

The fry starts to head downstream. It swims in a school, or large group, with hundreds of other fry. Some of them are eaten by larger fish, such as pike, sturgeon or even other salmon.

Sink or swim

Inside the fry's body is a sausage-shaped balloon – its swim bladder. This fills with air the first time the fry swims. The swim bladder allows the fish to keep at a certain level in the water, without sinking to the bottom or floating to the surface. The salmon can squeeze or relax it in order to float or sink in the water.

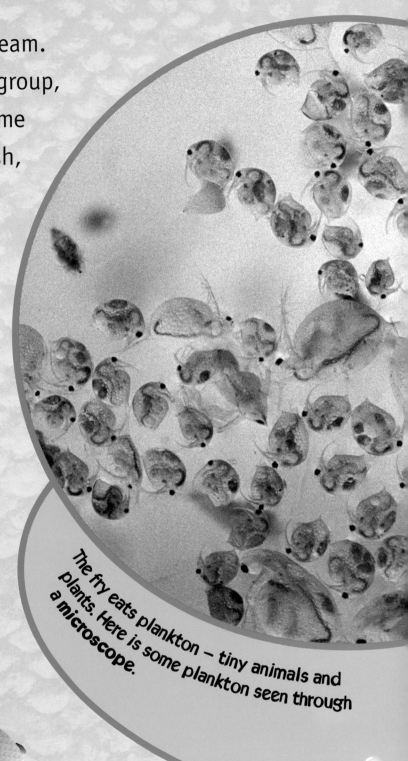

The fry eats plankton – tiny animals and plants. Here is some plankton seen through a microscope.

Spots and marks

As the **fry** grows, spots and stripes appear on its body. These are called **parr** marks, and the fish is now known as a parr. The markings help to **camouflage**, or hide, the fish among the weeds. They make it harder for hunters, or **predators**, to spot the fish. Herons and other water birds like to feed on parrs.

As a parr, the young salmon develops marks on its skin that help it to hide from predators.

Growing and eating

By now, the salmon is about 7 centimetres long. As well as insects, its diet includes shrimp, tadpoles and fish eggs. The parr has an amazing appetite! It stays in the river for months or even years, growing bigger and stronger.

Slime

The salmon's body is covered in a thin layer of slime, or mucus. This helps to protect its scales if the fish rubs against sharp stones on the river bed. The slime also makes the fish slippery – harder for a predator to catch!

The parrs dart about the stream, hunting for food.

Silvery smolt

When it is one to three years old, the salmon loses its brown parr marks. At this stage of its life, the salmon is called a **smolt**. Now it has silvery sides, a blueish-green back and a pale belly. Its new colouring will give excellent **camouflage** in the open ocean.

The smolt looks a bit like an adult salmon, only much smaller.

Water worlds

The smolt is about 15 centimetres long, but it is not quite ready for life at sea. Until now, it has been used to living in fresh water. Its body is going to have to make some big changes before it will be able to cope with the salty sea water.

From its lookout, a cormorant watches for movements in the water. It catches all sorts of fish to eat, including young salmon.

Attack from the air

Birds such as terns, gulls and cormorants head inland to swoop down and catch smolts that are swimming towards the sea. These awesome sea birds gobble millions of the young fish. An adult cormorant may gorge itself on more than one hundred smolts in a single feeding session!

Adapting to salt

The place where a river meets the sea is called an **estuary**. Estuary water is **brackish** – a mix of fresh water from the river and salt water from the sea.

This photograph of a river mouth, or estuary, was taken from the air. Salty sea water mixes with the river water when the tide comes in.

Getting ready

The **smolt** stays in the estuary for a few weeks or even months, getting used to the saltier water. The fish has a kidney inside its body that deals with waste. This **adapts** to cope with the extra salt. There are changes to the smolt's **gills**, too. The smolt needs to adapt slowly – but not all smolts get the chance. If the river floods, they might be washed out to sea before their bodies are ready. If this happens, the smolts die.

Waders

The smolt sticks to shallow wetlands around the edge of the estuary, where it is less likely to be washed out to sea. There are dangers here, too. Wading birds such as herons stalk the marshes, hoping to spear fish with their sharp beaks.

This poor fish has ended up in a kingfisher's beak.

Life at sea

Now the salmon leaves the **estuary** and begins its life at sea. It will stay in the ocean for the next one to eight years – until it is fully grown.

Hunter and hunted

There is more food in the ocean than there was in the estuary, so the salmon grows very quickly. It relies on its senses of smell and sight to find food, such as small fish, shrimp and squid.

Out at sea, the salmon hunt together in schools.

At the same time, the salmon must avoid becoming someone else's meal. Fishing boats drop their nets to catch salmon, and there are animal **predators**, too, including seals, sea lions and killer whales.

Marine mammals

Although they live in the sea, killer whales, sea lions and seals are closer relatives to you than to fish! Like you, they are **mammals**. They dive deep to hunt, but they need to come up to the surface every twenty minutes or so to breathe air.

The harbour seal is a swift hunter. Its diet includes salmon and other fish.

All grown up

Most salmon spend three or four years at sea, although some stay for up to eight years. During this time, the fish swims thousands of kilometres searching for good feeding grounds. Some salmon grow as long as 1.5 metres, though others reach only about 50 centimetres.

Fully-grown salmon are large fish and powerful swimmers.

Back to the river mouth

Once the salmon is fully grown, it is ready to have young. It finds its way back to the **estuary** where it first entered the sea. The salmon stays in the estuary while its body **adapts** to the **brackish** water, which has less salt than the sea water. When its body has changed enough to cope with fresh water, the salmon heads upriver.

Finding the way

No one knows exactly how the salmon finds its way back to its home stream. It may be that the fish recognizes different rivers and estuaries by their scent – and smells its way home!

Salmon that are ready to mate make their way back to the estuary.

Heading home

Travelling upstream is hard work. The salmon's body is large and strong, though. It is powerful enough to swim against the **current**. Even a small waterfall is not a problem. The salmon flings itself out of the water and splash-lands on the higher level. The salmon does not stop to feed. It lives off stored fats in its body. All its efforts go into the journey.

Salmon can hurl themselves up and over a mini waterfall.

Bold and bright

As it swims, the salmon changes colour. The male's colouring is bolder than the female's. He may be green, brown, lilac or red. This will help him to attract a female at the **spawning ground**.

Danger!

Predators have been waiting for the **salmon run**. Wild cats, wolves, bears and eagles visit the river. The fish face danger from human fishing, too.

Grizzly bears wait with jaws open, ready to snatch the leaping salmon.

Nests of eggs

At the **spawning ground**, the male and female salmon pair up. The female uses her tail to dig a shallow **redd** in the gravel. Then she pushes her back fin down into the redd and begins to lay her eggs. The male swims alongside and spreads his **sperm**, which is called milt, over the eggs to **fertilize** them.

The female waits for a male to swim up. He will fertilize her eggs as she drops them into the redd.

Thousands of eggs!

Using her tail, the female covers the redd and then starts to dig another. The salmon pair continue to dig and **spawn** until the female has used up all her eggs. Depending on her size, she can lay between 2500 and 7000 eggs.

A fish ladder like this one allows spawning salmon to make their way past a dam.

Finding a way

Dams are useful for people, but they block the way to spawning grounds and stop salmon finding the right conditions to lay eggs. At some dams, though, people have built fish ladders. These are stepped pools that allow the salmon to swim up the side of the dam.

Worn out

After they have **spawned**, the male and female salmon are weak and worn out. The long journey upstream has used up all their energy. They guard the **redd** for a few days, but soon die of tiredness. The dead fish feed many animals – perhaps even the new **fry** when they head downstream in a few months time!

Dying or dead salmon make an easy meal for animals such as this mink.

Starting again

A few types of salmon do not always die after spawning. They rest for a while and then head back downstream. When they reach the **estuary**, they wait while their bodies get used to the salt again. Then they return to the ocean, where there is plenty to eat.

Male sockeye salmon are a beautiful red colour. They often die after their amazing journey from the Pacific Ocean to spawn.

Salmon farms

Not all salmon live their whole lives in the wild. At salmon hatcheries, eggs and milt are collected from adult salmon that have been caught. The baby salmon are raised at the hatchery, out of reach of **predators**, then released into the wild. Salmon farms are different. Here, adult salmon are raised for food in cages out at sea.

Find out for yourself

The best way to find out more about the **life cycle** of a fish is to keep your own. You cannot keep pet salmon but you can keep goldfish – and they may even lay eggs! You can also find out more by visiting aquariums, reading books about salmon and other fish and by looking for information on the Internet.

Books to read

From Egg to Adult: The Life Cycle of a Fish, Louise and Richard Spilsbury (Heinemann Library, 2003)

The Life Cycle of a Salmon, Lisa Trumbauer and Thomas P. Quinn (Pebble Books/Capstone, 2003)

Worldlife Library: Salmon, John Baxter (Voyageur Press, 2002)

Using the Internet

Explore the Internet to find out more about salmon. Websites can change, but if one of the links below no longer works, don't worry. Use a search engine, such as www.yahooligans.com, and type in keywords such as 'salmon', '**alevin**', '**smolt**' and 'life cycle'.

Websites

http://www.enchantedlearning.com/subjects/fish/printouts/salmon.shtml
Learn more about salmon and print out pictures to colour in and keep.
http://www.jsd.k12.ak.us/ab/jones_cl/jones.htm
Take a look at this class project from a school in Alaska – all about the life cycle of salmon.

Glossary

adapt slowly change to cope with new conditions

alevin newly-hatched salmon that is still living in its redd

brackish water with some salt in it

camouflage colouring or marks on an animal that match its surroundings, making it hard for predators to spot

current flow of water moving in one direction

dam place where a river has been blocked

embryo baby animal before it has hatched from an egg or been born

estuary lowest part of a river where it meets the sea

fertilize join together male and female parts to create the beginnings of a new living thing

fry young river salmon that has absorbed its yolk sac, but not yet developed parr marks

gills special body parts under slits on either side of a fish's head. Gills allow fish to take oxygen out of the water to breathe.

life cycle all the different stages in the life of a living thing such as an animal or plant

mammal animal that gives birth to live young and feeds them milk

microscopic describes something so small that it can be seen only with the help of a microscope

migrate journey from one habitat, or place, to another at a particular time of year

oxygen gas in the air that living things need to breathe to stay alive

parr young river salmon that is between the fry and smolt stages and has camouflage markings

predator animal that hunts other animals and eats them for food

redd gravel nest where a salmon lays its eggs

salmon run journey of salmon to their spawning grounds

smolt young river salmon that has silvery sides and a blueish-green back

spawn reproduce. When the female lays her eggs and the male covers them with milt to fertilize them.

spawning ground place where a salmon goes to spawn

sperm male sex cells

yolk sac food attached to the body of a newly-hatched salmon, or alevin

Index

Titles in the *Life Cycles* series include:

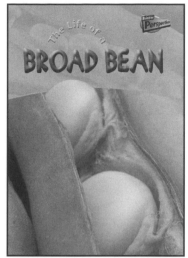

Hardback   1 844 43314 5

Hardback   1 844 43315 3

Hardback   1 844 43317 X

Hardback   1 844 43316 1

Hardback   1 844 43318 8

Hardback   1 844 43319 6

Find out about the other titles in this series on our website www.raintreepublishers.co.uk